600 AMAZING HOCKEY FACTS FOR YOUNG READERS

GERRY BIRD

Dedication

For all the young players and fans who bring energy, curiosity, and a love for the game to every rink, street, and backyard. May these stories inspire you to play with heart, cheer with passion, and dream big—on and off the ice.

Table of Contents

Introduction

Welcome to the world of ice hockey!

This book is packed with **600 amazing facts** about hockey, from record-breaking goals and famous players to quirky superstitions and legendary teams. Whether you're a new fan or already know your slap shots from your hat tricks, there's something here for everyone who loves the thrill of the ice.

Each page will take you deeper into the game, uncovering the skills, stories, and surprises that make hockey one of the most exciting sports on the planet. So, lace up your skates, grab your stick, and get ready to hit the ice!

Chapter 1: Fun Hockey Trivia

1. **"Did you know?"** The fastest recorded hockey puck shot zipped through the air at 118 miles per hour! That's almost as fast as a race car on the track.

2. **"Hockey's Icy Beginning"**: Ice hockey is over 150 years old and was first played outdoors on frozen ponds. Imagine how cold those games must've been!

3. **Zamboni Magic**: The Zamboni isn't just fun to watch; it's essential for smoothing out the ice. Without it, players would be skating over rough, bumpy ice, making the game much harder.

4. **Hockey Puck Fun Fact**: Ever wonder why a hockey puck is black? It's easier to see on the white ice—and at 1 inch thick, it's heavy enough to whiz through the air but small enough to slip past a goalie.

5. **Superstitions on the Ice**: Some players have quirky superstitions, like always putting on their left skate first or eating spaghetti before every game. Hockey players believe these little rituals help them play better!

6. **Goalie Gear Galore**: Did you know a goalie's gear can weigh up to 50 pounds? Those pads keep them protected when pucks are flying at high speeds.

7. **Guess What?** Hockey pucks are frozen before games so they don't bounce! Imagine trying to control a bouncing puck at 100 miles per hour.

8. **Hockey Mascots**: Every NHL team has its own mascot, from Gritty in Philadelphia to Gnash in Nashville. These mascots cheer, dance, and pump up the crowd during games!

9. **"Can you believe it?"** Some hockey sticks are made from carbon fiber, which is super strong and used to

make things like jet planes. Talk about high-tech equipment!

10. **"The Big Chill"**: An ice hockey rink is kept at around 16°F (-9°C) to keep the ice solid. That's colder than most home freezers!

11. **Goalie Pads Rule**: In the early days of hockey, goalies wore almost no padding. Today's goalies wear high-tech gear that keeps them safe—and some pads are custom-designed for each player.

12. **Penalty Time**: When players break a rule, they get sent to the "sin bin" or penalty box for a time-out, sometimes for up to five minutes.

13. **Record Puck Speed**: The hardest shot ever recorded in hockey? A blistering 118.3 mph by Russian player Alexander Ryazantsev in 2012.

14. **Sneaky Puck Facts**: Over 12,000 hockey pucks are used each season in the NHL. Sometimes pucks even get launched over the glass into the crowd!

15. **Rinks All Around**: Ice hockey is played on rinks all over the world—even in countries where it doesn't snow, like Thailand!

16. **Stanley Cup Travels**: The Stanley Cup, hockey's biggest prize, travels all over the world each year. Every player on the winning team gets to spend a day with it—some even take it swimming!

17. **Longest Game Ever**: The longest hockey game ever lasted 176 minutes—almost six hours of playtime! Now that's endurance.

18. **Unique Names**: Hockey has some funny names for plays and rules. There's "the five-hole" (the gap between a goalie's legs) and the "hat trick" (when a player scores three goals in one game).

19. **The Puck Drop**: Every hockey game starts with a face-off, where the referee drops the puck between two players. The fastest player to react gets control of the puck for their team!

20. **Hockey's Nicknames**: Hockey players have tons of nicknames, from "The Great One" (Wayne Gretzky) to "Sid the Kid" (Sidney Crosby). These names make the game even more memorable.

Chapter 2: Greatest Hockey Players

1. **Wayne Gretzky - "The Great One"**: Wayne Gretzky is widely known as the greatest hockey player of all time. He holds more records than any other player in NHL history, including scoring over 200 points in a single season four times!

2. **Super Mario**: Mario Lemieux, nicknamed "Super Mario," overcame injuries and even cancer to become

one of hockey's top scorers. He once returned to the ice on the same day he finished his last radiation treatment.

3. **Sid the Kid**: Sidney Crosby started making waves in the NHL at only 18 years old! He became the youngest player to score 100 points in a season.

4. **The Finnish Flash**: Teemu Selanne, known as the "Finnish Flash," scored 76 goals in his rookie year—a record that no one has broken yet!

5. **Jaromir Jagr**: With his famous mullet and incredible skill, Jagr played in the NHL for over 24 seasons, making him one of the oldest and most experienced players in the game.

6. **Rocket Richard**: Maurice "Rocket" Richard was the first player to score 50 goals in a season. His speed and accuracy earned him the nickname "Rocket."

7. **Alex Ovechkin's Power Shots**: Alex Ovechkin, one of the most powerful shooters in the NHL, has scored over 800 goals. He's often called one of the best pure goal-scorers in hockey.

8. **Mark Messier - The Leader**: Known for his leadership, Mark Messier captained two different teams to Stanley Cup victories, and he's one of only a few players to do that!

9. **Mr. Hockey**: Gordie Howe, known as "Mr. Hockey," played professionally for five decades! He could score, fight, and pass better than most.

10. **The Golden Jet**: Bobby Hull was called "The Golden Jet" for his incredible speed on the ice and his powerful slap shot, which was one of the hardest shots in hockey.

11. **Henrik "King" Lundqvist**: Known as "The King," Lundqvist was one of the top goalies of his time, especially loved by fans of the New York Rangers.

12. **Joe Sakic's Wrist Shot**: Joe Sakic had one of the best wrist shots in the NHL. He led the Colorado Avalanche to two Stanley Cup wins and was famous for his speed and accuracy.

13. **Bobby Orr - The Flying Defenseman**: Orr changed how defensemen play the game, often skating all the way up to the net and scoring himself.

14. **The Big Z - Zdeno Chara**: Standing at 6'9", Chara is the tallest player to ever play in the NHL. His height gives him an advantage with his powerful slap shot and defensive skills.

15. **Steve Yzerman - The Captain**: Steve Yzerman, captain of the Detroit Red Wings for 20 years, led his team to three Stanley Cups with his hard work and dedication.

16. **The Russian Rocket - Pavel Bure**: Pavel Bure was known for his blazing speed, earning him the nickname "The Russian Rocket." Watching him zoom across the ice was always a thrill.

17. **Patrick Roy - The Butterfly Goalie**: Patrick Roy was known for his "butterfly" style, where he would drop to his knees to block low shots. He's one of the best goalies in history.

18. **Connor McDavid - The Speedster**: Connor McDavid is known for his lightning-fast speed and agility. Many say he's the fastest player in the NHL today!

19. **Jean Beliveau's Class**: Jean Beliveau was not only a skilled player but also known for his classy, respectful attitude, earning him fans and admiration worldwide.

20. **Datsyuk the Magician**: Pavel Datsyuk, often called "The Magician," was famous for his unbelievable stick-handling skills. He could deke around anyone on the ice!

Chapter 3: The Stanley Cup

1. **Oldest Trophy in Sports**: The Stanley Cup is over 125 years old, making it the oldest trophy in North American sports.

2. **A Royal Gift**: The Cup was donated by Lord Stanley of Preston, a Canadian governor, who wanted to inspire young players to love the sport.

3. **Names on the Cup**: Every player from the winning team has their name engraved on the Cup, making each victory part of hockey history.

4. **A Cup of Adventures**: The Stanley Cup has traveled around the world—from Russia to Mexico. Each player on the winning team gets a day with the Cup.

5. **The Curious Dents**: The Stanley Cup has been dropped, dented, and even chipped over the years. It's been through a lot!

6. **Champions Only**: The Cup is only awarded to the best team of the season, so not all players get a chance to hold it in their careers.

7. **The Cup That Swims**: Some players have even taken the Cup swimming or on a boat ride, like when the Tampa Bay Lightning took it out on the water!

8. **Superstitions Galore**: Many players refuse to touch the Stanley Cup unless they win it. They believe touching it beforehand is bad luck.

9. **The Cup on the Ice**: After a team wins, the Cup is brought right onto the ice so the players can lift it up in celebration.

10. **Family Names**: The Cup has family names engraved multiple times, as many players have had sons or brothers who also won it.

11. **The Cup Travels in Style**: When the Cup travels, it has its own special case and security team. It's treated like a real VIP!

12. **Famous Engravings**: Some names on the Cup were actually misspelled, and once they realized, they simply crossed them out!

13. **The Missing Rings**: Every 13 years, they add a new ring to the base of the Cup to make space for more names. The old rings are kept safe in the Hall of Fame.

14. **International Influence**: The Cup has names from over 20 different countries, showing how worldwide the love for hockey has become.

15. **The Cup's Big Break**: In 2005, the Cup wasn't awarded due to a lockout season—the only year it stayed in the Hall of Fame instead of with a winning team.

16. **Stanley Cup Parades**: Every year, the winning team hosts a huge parade with the Cup, showing it off to their fans and celebrating their victory.

17. **Feeding Frenzy**: Players have eaten all kinds of food out of the Cup, from cereal and pasta to champagne and even dog food (for their pets, of course!).

18. **Stanley's First Journey**: When the Cup was first awarded, it wasn't as big and fancy. It started as a simple bowl that players would take home.

19. **A Cup for Kids**: The Stanley Cup even makes appearances at children's hospitals, bringing smiles to young fans around the world.

20. **The Keeper of the Cup**: There's a special person called the "Keeper of the Cup" who protects and cares for it year-round, making sure it stays in top condition.

Chapter 4: Famous Hockey Rivalries

1. **Canada vs. USA**: This rivalry is fierce, especially during the Olympics! When these two teams face off, fans from both sides are on the edge of their seats.

2. **Maple Leafs vs. Canadiens**: The Toronto Maple Leafs and Montreal Canadiens have the longest-running rivalry in hockey. These Canadian teams have been battling it out since 1917!

3. **Battle of Alberta**: The Calgary Flames and Edmonton Oilers compete in what's known as the "Battle of Alberta." Their games are intense and physical, with fans cheering wildly.

4. **Red Wings vs. Avalanche**: In the '90s, the Detroit Red Wings and Colorado Avalanche had one of the fiercest rivalries, with fights, hard hits, and unforgettable moments.

5. **Penguins vs. Flyers**: Known as the "Battle of Pennsylvania," the Pittsburgh Penguins and Philadelphia Flyers rivalry brings out tons of emotions—and penalties!

6. **Rangers vs. Islanders**: The New York Rangers and New York Islanders rivalry is a classic. Whenever they play, it's a battle for bragging rights in New York!

7. **Bruins vs. Canadiens**: The Boston Bruins and Montreal Canadiens rivalry dates back to the early days of the NHL, making it one of the most heated in history.

8. **Blackhawks vs. Blues**: When the Chicago Blackhawks play the St. Louis Blues, fans expect a rough,

competitive game. These teams have been rivals since the 1970s!

9. **Sharks vs. Kings**: The rivalry between the San Jose Sharks and Los Angeles Kings keeps California hockey fans buzzing with excitement.

10. **Oilers vs. Kings**: This rivalry took off when Wayne Gretzky was traded from the Oilers to the Kings in 1988, shocking hockey fans and sparking intense games.

11. **Canucks vs. Flames**: The Vancouver Canucks and Calgary Flames rivalry often leads to heated exchanges and memorable moments, especially in the playoffs.

12. **Flyers vs. Devils**: The Philadelphia Flyers and New Jersey Devils rivalry sees lots of close games and hard hits, making each game unpredictable.

13. **Senators vs. Leafs**: The Ottawa Senators and Toronto Maple Leafs rivalry, often called the "Battle of Ontario," fires up fans across Canada.

14. **Red Wings vs. Blackhawks**: Two of the NHL's oldest teams, the Detroit Red Wings and Chicago Blackhawks, have a respectful but fierce rivalry.

15. **Wild vs. Avalanche**: The rivalry between the Minnesota Wild and Colorado Avalanche adds extra excitement for fans in the Midwest.

16. **Flames vs. Oilers**: Another Battle of Alberta matchup, the Flames and Oilers are known for their physical games and passionate fans.

17. **Sabres vs. Maple Leafs**: When Buffalo plays Toronto, it's a showdown at the border, with fans crossing over to cheer on their teams.

18. **Kings vs. Ducks**: Known as the "Freeway Face-Off," the Los Angeles Kings and Anaheim Ducks rivalry is a big deal in California.

19. **Stars vs. Predators**: The Dallas Stars and Nashville Predators rivalry has grown in recent years, with both teams fighting for a spot in the playoffs.

20. **Rangers vs. Devils**: The rivalry between the New York Rangers and New Jersey Devils always delivers exciting games, with both teams competing for local pride.

Chapter 5: Scoring Records

1. **Gretzky's 2,857 Points**: Wayne Gretzky holds the record for the most points in NHL history—2,857! This record is so high that no player has come close to breaking it.

2. **Most Goals in a Season**: Wayne Gretzky also holds the record for the most goals in a single season—92 goals in 1981-82!

3. **Fastest Hat Trick**: Bill Mosienko scored three goals in just 21 seconds in 1952, setting the record for the fastest hat trick in NHL history.

4. **Most Points in One Game**: Darryl Sittler scored 10 points in a single game in 1976, a record that still stands today.

5. **Youngest to Score 50 Goals**: Wayne Gretzky was only 19 when he became the youngest player to score 50 goals in a season.

6. **Oldest Goal Scorer**: Gordie Howe scored a goal at 52, showing that age is just a number in hockey!

7. **Most Goals in a Career**: Wayne Gretzky again holds this record with 894 goals in his career.

8. **Most Assists in a Season**: Gretzky set the record for assists in a season with 163 in 1985-86, a record that has yet to be matched.

9. **Fastest to 500 Goals**: Gretzky scored his 500th goal in just 575 games, making him the fastest to reach this milestone.

10. **50 Goals in 39 Games**: In the 1981-82 season, Gretzky scored 50 goals in just 39 games—a feat no one else has achieved.

11. **Most Goals in a Playoff Season**: Reggie Leach scored 19 goals in the 1975-76 playoffs, setting a record for postseason goals.

12. **Most Points by a Defenseman**: Paul Coffey scored 48 goals as a defenseman in 1985-86, an impressive record for a non-forward player.

13. **Most Career Playoff Points**: Gretzky also holds the record for the most playoff points, with 382.

14. **Most Career Points for a Defenseman**: Ray Bourque holds the record for most career points by a defenseman with 1,579.

15. **Most Consecutive 50-Goal Seasons**: Mike Bossy and Wayne Gretzky share the record with nine consecutive 50-goal seasons each.

16. **Most Goals in One Period**: Joe Malone scored seven goals in one period in 1920—a record that still holds today.

17. **Most Goals in a Single Playoff Game**: Newsy Lalonde scored six goals in one playoff game in 1919.

18. **Most Game-Winning Goals**: Jaromir Jagr has the record for the most game-winning goals, with 135.

19. **Most Points in a Rookie Season**: Teemu Selanne scored 132 points in his rookie year, including 76 goals, setting the bar high for newcomers.

20. **Highest Goals Per Game Average**: Joe Malone has the highest goals-per-game average, scoring 2.2 goals per game during the 1917-18 season.

Chapter 6: Legendary Teams

1. **The Montreal Canadiens Dynasty**: The Canadiens won five consecutive Stanley Cups from 1956 to 1960, one of the longest winning streaks in NHL history.

2. **Edmonton Oilers of the '80s**: With players like Wayne Gretzky and Mark Messier, the Oilers dominated the 1980s, winning five Stanley Cups.

3. **New York Islanders Streak**: The Islanders won four consecutive Stanley Cups from 1980 to 1983, making them one of the most successful teams of the early '80s.

4. **Detroit Red Wings' Long Playoff Streak**: The Red Wings made the playoffs for 25 straight years, from 1991 to 2016, a remarkable feat of consistency.

5. **Chicago Blackhawks' 2010s Comeback**: After years without a championship, the Blackhawks won three Stanley Cups in six years, in 2010, 2013, and 2015.

6. **The Big Bad Bruins**: In the 1970s, the Boston Bruins were known for their physical play and powerful players like Bobby Orr and Phil Esposito.

7. **Pittsburgh Penguins in the '90s**: With stars like Mario Lemieux and Jaromir Jagr, the Penguins won back-to-back Stanley Cups in 1991 and 1992.

8. **Broad Street Bullies**: The 1970s Philadelphia Flyers earned this nickname for their rough style of play, winning two Stanley Cups.

9. **Colorado Avalanche's Strong Start**: After relocating to Colorado, the Avalanche won their first Stanley Cup in 1996 and added another in 2001.

10. **Toronto Maple Leafs' Early Success**: One of the original teams in the NHL, the Maple Leafs have a rich history with 13 Stanley Cups.

11. **The St. Louis Blues' First Win**: In 2019, the Blues won their first Stanley Cup after 52 years in the league.

12. **Dallas Stars' Texas Triumph**: The Stars won their first Stanley Cup in 1999, making them the pride of Texas hockey.

13. **The Kings of LA**: The Los Angeles Kings brought hockey glory to California with Stanley Cup wins in 2012 and 2014.

14. **New Jersey Devils in the 2000s**: Known for their strong defense, the Devils won three Stanley Cups between 1995 and 2003.

15. **Winnipeg Jets Return**: After the original Jets left for Arizona, Winnipeg got its team back in 2011, and the fans welcomed them with open arms.

16. **Golden Knights' Historic First Season**: The Vegas Golden Knights reached the Stanley Cup Finals in their debut season, an incredible feat for a new team.

17. **Ottawa Senators' Early Days**: The Senators won several Stanley Cups in the 1920s, making them one of the earliest successful teams.

18. **The Mighty Ducks**: Known for their Disney-inspired beginnings, the Anaheim Ducks made a surprising run to win the Stanley Cup in 2007.

19. **The Hartford Whalers**: Although they moved to become the Carolina Hurricanes, the Whalers still have a loyal fanbase who remember their iconic logo and colors.

20. **Buffalo Sabres' Fan Base**: Though they've never won the Cup, the Sabres' fans are some of the most loyal in the league, always cheering for their team.

Chapter 7: Top Scoring Moments

1. **Gretzky's 50 Goals in 39 Games**: In 1981, Wayne Gretzky scored 50 goals in just 39 games, a record that still stands today. It's one of the most famous scoring streaks in hockey history.

2. **The 1993 Playoff Explosion**: In the 1993 playoffs, Mario Lemieux, Wayne Gretzky, and Doug Gilmour led an explosion of goals, with multiple high-scoring games that kept fans on the edge of their seats.

3. **Rocket Richard's 50 in 50**: Maurice "Rocket" Richard was the first player to score 50 goals in 50 games back in 1945, setting a standard that inspired generations of goal-scorers.

4. **Lemieux's Five Goals, Five Ways**: Mario Lemieux scored five goals in one game—each in a different way! Even-strength, power-play, short-handed, penalty shot, and an empty-net goal.

5. **Joe Sakic's Clutch Playoff Goals**: Known as "Captain Clutch," Sakic scored 18 game-winning goals in the playoffs, proving his ability to perform under pressure.

6. **Ovechkin's 500th Goal**: Alex Ovechkin hit the 500-goal mark in 2016 with a powerful shot, becoming one of the youngest players to reach this milestone.

7. **Bossy's 50 Goals in 50 Games**: Mike Bossy joined Rocket Richard in the elite "50 in 50" club in 1981, scoring 50 goals in the Islanders' first 50 games of the season.

8. **McDavid's Four-Goal Debut**: In his debut game, Connor McDavid scored four goals, immediately making his mark as a top player.

9. **The Great One's 802nd Goal**: Wayne Gretzky scored his 802nd goal in 1994, passing Gordie Howe to become the all-time leading goal-scorer.

10. **Jarome Iginla's 600 Goals**: Iginla scored his 600th career goal in 2016, making him one of the few players to hit this impressive milestone.

11. **Jagr's 1,888 Points**: Jaromir Jagr scored his 1,888th point in 2017, solidifying his place as one of the NHL's highest-scoring players.

12. **Teemu Selanne's Record Rookie Season**: In his first year, Selanne scored 76 goals, setting a rookie record that has yet to be broken.

13. **Darryl Sittler's 10-Point Game**: Sittler scored 10 points in a single game in 1976, including six goals and four assists—a record no one has matched.

14. **Bobby Hull's 54 Goals**: Bobby Hull became the first player to score more than 50 goals in a season, with 54 goals in 1965-66.

15. **Crosby's "Golden Goal"**: Sidney Crosby scored the game-winning goal in overtime to give Canada the gold

medal in the 2010 Olympics—one of the most celebrated goals in Canadian hockey history.

16. **Phil Esposito's 76 Goals in 1970-71**: Esposito set a new single-season record with 76 goals, a feat that inspired young hockey players everywhere.

17. **Brett Hull's 86 Goals**: Brett Hull scored 86 goals in the 1990-91 season, making him one of the highest goal-scorers in a single season.

18. **Pavel Bure's 60-Goal Seasons**: The "Russian Rocket" scored over 60 goals in two different seasons, showcasing his speed and scoring ability.

19. **Henrik Sedin's 112-Point Season**: Sedin led the league in scoring in 2010 with 112 points, proving he was one of the best playmakers in the game.

20. **Lafleur's 50 Goals, 100 Points Seasons**: Guy Lafleur was the first player to have six straight seasons with at least 50 goals and 100 points, making him a scoring legend.

Chapter 8: Olympic Hockey

1. **Miracle on Ice**: In 1980, the U.S. Olympic team defeated the heavily favored Soviet team in a game known as the "Miracle on Ice." This win is one of the most famous moments in sports history.

2. **Canada's Golden Goal**: Sidney Crosby's overtime goal in 2010 brought Canada the gold medal, sending Canadian fans into a frenzy.

3. **Women's Hockey Debut**: Women's ice hockey was added to the Olympics in 1998, and the USA won the first gold medal, marking a huge moment for women's sports.

4. **First Olympic Hockey Game**: The first Olympic hockey game was held in 1920, and Canada won the gold medal, showing the world their hockey prowess.

5. **Soviet Domination**: The Soviet Union dominated Olympic hockey for years, winning seven gold medals between 1956 and 1988.

6. **NHL Players in the Olympics**: In 1998, the NHL allowed its players to participate in the Olympics for the first time, leading to some of the most competitive games ever.

7. **Finnish Pride**: Finland has a strong history in Olympic hockey, with their women's and men's teams consistently winning medals.

8. **Sweden's Double Gold**: Sweden's men's team won Olympic gold in 1994 and 2006, establishing themselves as one of the top hockey nations.

9. **Japanese Women's Team**: Japan's women's team, known as "Smile Japan," inspired fans worldwide with their joy and team spirit in the 2018 Olympics.

10. **Ice Rink Size Difference**: Olympic ice rinks are larger than NHL rinks, giving players more room to skate and pass.

11. **Great Britain's Surprise Gold**: In 1936, Great Britain won an unexpected gold medal, showing that hockey talent exists outside North America.

12. **Record-Breaking Gold**: Canada holds the record for the most Olympic gold medals in men's hockey, proving their dominance on the world stage.

13. **Germany's Surprise Silver**: In 2018, Germany shocked the world by reaching the finals and winning a silver medal against the Olympic Athletes from Russia.

14. **Jarome Iginla's Olympic Heroics**: Iginla was instrumental in Canada's gold medal win in 2002, especially with his play in the final game.

15. **Russia's 2018 Gold**: In 2018, the Olympic Athletes from Russia won gold after defeating Germany in overtime, ending their Olympic gold drought.

16. **Women's Rivalry - USA vs. Canada**: The USA and Canada women's teams have a heated rivalry in Olympic hockey, with close games that keep fans on the edge of their seats.

17. **Youthful Medalists**: In 1924, a 17-year-old Canadian player became the youngest hockey gold medalist in Olympic history.

18. **NHL Stars in Nagano**: The 1998 Winter Olympics in Nagano, Japan, was the first time NHL stars like Wayne Gretzky and Dominik Hasek competed, making it a historic tournament.

19. **Highest-Scoring Game**: In 1924, Canada defeated Switzerland 33-0 in one of the highest-scoring games in Olympic history!

20. **First Overtime Gold**: In 1994, Sweden and Canada went to a shootout in the gold medal game, with Sweden winning the first-ever Olympic hockey game decided in overtime.

Chapter 9: Record-Breaking Games

1. **Longest NHL Game Ever**: In 1936, the Detroit Red Wings and Montreal Maroons played the longest game in NHL history—176 minutes and 30 seconds!

2. **Most Goals in a Game**: In 1920, the Montreal Canadiens scored a record 16 goals in one game against the Quebec Bulldogs.

3. **Highest Scoring NHL Game**: In 1985, the Edmonton Oilers and Chicago Blackhawks combined for 21 goals in a single game, with Edmonton winning 12-9.

4. **Largest Winning Margin**: Canada beat Denmark 47-0 in the 1949 World Championship, a record-setting score.

5. **Most Points by One Team**: The Montreal Canadiens scored a record-breaking 132 points in the 1976-77 season, a record that remains unbroken.

6. **Most Shutouts in a Season**: George Hainsworth recorded 22 shutouts in a single season in 1928-29, setting an incredible record for goaltending.

7. **Most Goals in an International Game**: Canada scored 33 goals in a single game against Switzerland at the 1924 Olympics.

8. **Highest Combined Score in a Playoff Game**: In 1982, the Calgary Flames and Los Angeles Kings combined for 18 goals in a playoff game.

9. **Fewest Shots in a Game**: In 1956, the Chicago Blackhawks took only eight shots in an entire game—a record low!

10. **The "Fog Game"**: In the 1975 playoffs, a thick fog filled the Buffalo Sabres' arena, creating a spooky and unforgettable game.

11. **Shortest Overtime Goal**: Brian Skrudland scored a goal 9 seconds into overtime in the 1986 playoffs, setting the record for the fastest playoff OT goal.

12. **Most Penalty Minutes in a Game**: The Boston Bruins and Minnesota North Stars combined for 406 penalty minutes in a single game in 1981!

13. **Most Goals in a Stanley Cup Final Game**: In 1982, the New York Islanders and Vancouver Canucks combined for 15 goals in a single Stanley Cup Final game.

14. **First Hat Trick in History**: In 1917, Harry Hyland scored the first-ever hat trick in NHL history with five goals in a game.

15. **The Easter Epic**: In 1987, the New York Islanders and Washington Capitals played a game that went into four overtimes, ending early on Easter morning.

16. **Fastest Goal in NHL History**: Doug Smail scored just 5 seconds into a game in 1981, setting the record for the fastest goal from the start.

17. **Biggest Comeback in Playoff History**: In 2011, the Philadelphia Flyers came back from being down 3 games to none in a series, winning four straight to beat the Boston Bruins.

18. **Fewest Goals Allowed in a Season**: The Montreal Canadiens allowed only 131 goals in the 1955-56 season, setting a defensive record.

19. **Highest Shots on Goal in One Game**: The Chicago Blackhawks took 92 shots on goal in a game against the Montreal Canadiens in 1941.

20. **Most Goals by a Rookie in a Game**: Joe Malone scored five goals in his NHL debut in 1917, setting a high bar for rookies.

Chapter 10: Superstitions and Rituals

1. **Left Skate First**: Many players, like Sidney Crosby, always put on their left skate before the right one, believing it brings good luck.

2. **Same Meal, Every Game**: Some players eat the same meal before every game. For Wayne Gretzky, it was a peanut butter and jelly sandwich!

3. **Patrick Roy Talks to Goalposts**: Legendary goalie Patrick Roy would talk to his goalposts, believing they were his "friends" protecting the net.

4. **The Playoff Beard**: Many players grow their beards out during the playoffs. This tradition started in the 1980s with the New York Islanders and is now a league-wide superstition.

5. **Touching the Ice**: Some players touch the ice with their stick as they enter the rink, feeling it connects them to the game.

6. **Bobby Orr's Skate Spin**: Orr had a unique ritual of spinning around on the ice during warm-ups. He felt it helped him "find his balance" before games.

7. **Don't Touch the Trophy**: Many players refuse to touch the conference championship trophy, believing it's bad luck to touch anything other than the Stanley Cup.

8. **Superstitious Socks**: Some players wear the same socks throughout the season, believing they bring luck—even if they're worn out and holey!

9. **Goalies' Special Moves**: Goalies often have specific routines, like tapping the posts in a certain order before each period.

10. **Same Pre-Game Song**: Many players listen to the same song before every game to get in the zone. For example, Alexander Ovechkin always listens to techno music.

11. **Secret Handshakes**: Some teammates create secret handshakes as part of their pre-game routine, a symbol of their close bond.

12. **Kissing the Stick**: Some players kiss their sticks before a big play, hoping it brings them luck on the ice.

13. **Don't Step on the Logo**: In many locker rooms, stepping on the team logo on the floor is considered bad luck, and players go out of their way to avoid it.

14. **Throwing Powder**: In the old days, players would sprinkle baby powder on their skates to make them feel lighter and faster.

15. **Taping Rituals**: Many players tape their sticks in a specific pattern every game. Some even insist on using a certain color tape.

16. **The Lucky Hat**: Some coaches and fans wear the same "lucky" hat throughout the playoffs, believing it will help their team win.

17. **Goalie "Stick Hug"**: Some goalies hug their sticks before each game, treating it like a lucky charm that will help them make saves.

18. **Secret Rituals**: Some players are so superstitious about their routines that they keep them a secret, afraid that sharing might ruin the magic.

19. **Routine Stretching**: Many players have specific stretching routines they believe keep them injury-free. Some even do these stretches at the exact same spot in the locker room!

20. **Goal Dance**: Some players have a "goal dance" they do in their heads whenever they score. It's a private celebration, even if no one else can see it.

Chapter 11: Youngest and Oldest Players

1. **Youngest NHL Player**: Bep Guidolin was just 16 years old when he played his first NHL game in 1942, making him the youngest player in league history.

2. **Oldest NHL Player**: Gordie Howe played his final NHL game at 52, proving that age was just a number for "Mr. Hockey."

3. **Connor McDavid's Early Start**: McDavid played his first NHL game at 18, but he'd been seen as a future superstar since his teenage years.

4. **Oldest Goalie**: Johnny Bower was still playing goalie for the Toronto Maple Leafs at age 45, making incredible saves in his final years.

5. **Youngest Goalie to Win the Stanley Cup**: Patrick Roy won his first Stanley Cup at age 20, becoming one of the youngest goalies to achieve this milestone.

6. **Wayne Gretzky's Early Success**: Gretzky joined the NHL at 18, and by the time he was 19, he had already broken records.

7. **Oldest Rookie**: Connie Madigan became the oldest rookie in NHL history at 38, showing it's never too late to chase your dreams.

8. **Youngest Stanley Cup Winner**: Larry Hillman won the Stanley Cup at 18, making him one of the youngest champions in league history.

9. **Oldest Player in the Playoffs**: Chris Chelios played in the playoffs at age 48, setting a record as one of the oldest players to compete.

10. **Youngest All-Star**: At just 18, Connor McDavid was named to the NHL All-Star Game, making waves as a teenage sensation.

11. **Oldest Hat Trick**: Gordie Howe scored a hat trick at age 41, making him the oldest player to achieve this feat.

12. **Youngest Hat Trick**: Jack Hamilton scored a hat trick at age 18, making him one of the youngest players to score three goals in one game.

13. **Oldest Goal Scorer**: Jaromir Jagr scored a goal at 45, showing that even in his 40s, he could still put the puck in the net.

14. **Youngest Captain**: At just 19, Gabriel Landeskog was named captain of the Colorado Avalanche, becoming the youngest team captain in NHL history.

15. **Oldest Team Captain**: Mark Messier was captain of the New York Rangers at 43, leading his team with experience and wisdom.

16. **Youngest Player to Reach 100 Points**: Sidney Crosby scored his 100th point at age 18, proving he was a prodigy.

17. **Oldest Player to Score in the Stanley Cup Finals**: In 2008, Chris Chelios scored in the Finals at age 46.

18. **Youngest Olympic Player**: At age 15, Rasmus Dahlin played for Sweden in the Olympics, making him one of the youngest players in Olympic history.

19. **Youngest Goalie to Play in NHL**: Harry Lumley played his first NHL game as a goalie at just 17, showing early on that he could compete with the pros.

20. **Youngest Player to Play in Stanley Cup Final**: Jarome Iginla played in his first Stanley Cup Final at age 19, marking the start of a legendary career.

Chapter 12: Zamboni Fun Facts

1. **The First Zamboni**: The first Zamboni was built in 1949 by Frank Zamboni. Before that, it took a team of people to resurface the ice!

2. **The Zamboni's Name**: The machine is named after its inventor, Frank Zamboni, who wanted to make a smoother and faster way to prepare the ice.

3. **It's Slow and Steady**: A Zamboni usually moves at about 9 miles per hour while resurfacing the ice—slow but steady!

4. **Water Magic**: The Zamboni uses hot water to resurface the ice because it fills cracks more smoothly than cold water.

5. **Zamboni in Every Arena**: Nearly every ice rink in the world has a Zamboni, making it an essential part of the game.

6. **The Ice Smoothness Secret**: A Zamboni shaves off a thin layer of ice before adding the new, smooth layer on top.

7. **It's Surprisingly Heavy**: A Zamboni can weigh up to 7,000 pounds—that's about the same as a car!

8. **Fuel Options**: Zambonis can run on various fuels, including propane, natural gas, and electric power, making them versatile machines.

9. **Zamboni Drivers Are Stars**: Some Zamboni drivers become famous in their cities, especially when fans cheer as they drive by.

10. **Zambonis Can Drift**: On turns, a Zamboni can actually slide or drift a bit, especially on very cold ice.

11. **Water Capacity**: A Zamboni can hold about 200 gallons of water in its tank, which is enough to resurface an entire rink.

12. **The Zamboni Wave**: Fans often wave at the Zamboni driver between periods, making it a fun tradition in hockey arenas.

13. **Zambonis in Movies**: The Zamboni has appeared in various movies and TV shows, becoming a pop culture icon.

14. **Zamboni Leagues**: Believe it or not, there are competitions and leagues where Zamboni drivers show off their ice-resurfacing skills.

15. **Eco-Friendly Zambonis**: Some rinks now use electric Zambonis, which don't produce exhaust and are better for the environment.

16. **Zamboni at the White House**: A Zamboni was once brought to the White House for a special winter event!

17. **Zamboni Time Limits**: Professional Zamboni drivers aim to resurface the ice in under 10 minutes to keep the game moving smoothly.

18. **Zamboni Training**: Driving a Zamboni isn't easy! Drivers go through special training to learn how to handle the machine on slippery ice.

19. **Zamboni Rides**: Some arenas offer Zamboni rides for fans, especially kids, who get a close-up view of how it works.

20. **A Zamboni Wedding**: One couple even got married on a Zamboni, proving that hockey fans will do anything to include the game in their big day!

Chapter 13: International Tournaments

1. **The World Championship**: The annual World Championship is one of hockey's biggest events, with teams from all over the world competing for the title.

2. **Canada's 27 Golds**: Canada holds the record for the most gold medals in World Championship history, showing their dominance in the sport.

3. **The "Big Six"**: The top six countries in international hockey are Canada, the USA, Russia, Sweden,

Finland, and the Czech Republic, and they often dominate tournaments.

4. **IIHF Women's World Championship**: This tournament, held since 1990, is the biggest event for women's international hockey, with the USA and Canada as the most successful teams.

5. **The Spengler Cup**: Held every December in Switzerland, the Spengler Cup is one of the oldest international tournaments, featuring club teams from different countries.

6. **Under-20 World Juniors**: The World Junior Championships showcase the best young players under 20, with future NHL stars often shining in this tournament.

7. **USA's Miracle Run**: The USA won their first World Championship gold in 1933, surprising everyone with their skill and determination.

8. **Russia's International Dominance**: Russia and the former Soviet Union have won numerous international tournaments, proving their strength in hockey.

9. **The Channel One Cup**: This Russian tournament, part of the Euro Hockey Tour, invites top European teams to compete in Moscow.

10. **Finland's Cinderella Story**: In 2019, Finland won the World Championship with a roster of mostly unknown players, defeating powerhouse teams along the way.

11. **The Karjala Tournament**: Held in Finland, this tournament is part of the Euro Hockey Tour and is a favorite for European hockey fans.

12. **Canada Cup to World Cup of Hockey**: The Canada Cup, later renamed the World Cup of Hockey, has featured top players from around the world since the 1970s.

13. **World Junior Rivalries**: The USA and Canada have one of the fiercest rivalries in the World Juniors, with games often coming down to the final seconds.

14. **The Gagarin Cup**: The KHL, Russia's top league, awards the Gagarin Cup to its champion, a trophy named after astronaut Yuri Gagarin.

15. **Sweden's Strong Showing**: Sweden has a rich history in international hockey, winning multiple World Championships and Olympic medals.

16. **The Euro Hockey Tour**: This tour features tournaments across Europe, with top teams from Sweden, Finland, Russia, and the Czech Republic.

17. **Germany's Rise**: Germany's silver medal at the 2018 Olympics shocked the hockey world, showing they are becoming a stronger team internationally.

18. **Youth Olympic Hockey**: The Youth Olympics showcase young talent, with players under 18 representing their countries on a global stage.

19. **The Four Nations Cup**: This annual women's tournament features teams from the USA, Canada, Sweden, and Finland, providing intense competition.

20. **The Great Britain Comeback**: After years away from top-level hockey, Great Britain returned to the World Championship in 2019, surprising fans and opponents alike.

Chapter 14: Hockey Leagues

1. **The NHL - North America's Finest**: The National Hockey League (NHL) is the top hockey league in North America, with teams in the USA and Canada.

2. **The AHL**: The American Hockey League (AHL) is the NHL's main development league, where young players gain experience before moving up.

3. **The KHL - Russia's Elite**: The Kontinental Hockey League (KHL) in Russia is one of the top leagues in Europe and features many former NHL players.

4. **Sweden's SHL**: The Swedish Hockey League (SHL) is one of Europe's most competitive leagues, producing many talented players.

5. **Finland's Liiga**: Known for its fast pace, Finland's Liiga has produced numerous NHL players, including some of the league's top goalies.

6. **Switzerland's National League**: Switzerland's league has grown in popularity and features players from around the world, including former NHL stars.

7. **The CHL - Canadian Juniors**: The Canadian Hockey League (CHL) includes three major junior leagues in Canada, showcasing young talent bound for the NHL.

8. **NCAA Hockey**: College hockey in the USA is growing fast, with NCAA teams producing many NHL players and even Olympic athletes.

9. **Germany's DEL**: The Deutsche Eishockey Liga (DEL) is Germany's top league, with a strong fan base and talented players.

10. **Czech Extraliga**: The top league in the Czech Republic, Extraliga is known for producing skilled players who often move on to the NHL or KHL.

11. **The WHL - Western Juniors**: The Western Hockey League (WHL) is one of Canada's top junior leagues, covering the western provinces and some U.S. states.

12. **Ontario Hockey League (OHL)**: The OHL is one of the CHL's three leagues, featuring top talent from Ontario and the U.S.

13. **The QMJHL**: The Quebec Major Junior Hockey League (QMJHL) focuses on players from Quebec and the Atlantic provinces, known for its high-scoring games.

14. **The EIHL**: The Elite Ice Hockey League (EIHL) is the UK's main league, with teams in England, Scotland, Wales, and Northern Ireland.

15. **Asia League Ice Hockey**: The Asia League includes teams from Japan, South Korea, and Russia, promoting hockey growth in Asia.

16. **The VHL**: The VHL, or Russian Major League, is a tier below the KHL and helps develop players for the top Russian league.

17. **The ECHL**: The ECHL in North America serves as a development league for the NHL and AHL, with teams in smaller cities.

18. **Norway's GET-ligaen**: Norway's top league, the GET-ligaen, is a smaller but growing league in European hockey.

19. **Austria's EBEL**: The Austrian Hockey League (EBEL) features teams from Austria, Italy, and other European countries.

20. **Slovakia's Tipsport Liga**: Slovakia's top league, the Tipsport Liga, has a rich history and many dedicated fans.

Chapter 15: Women's Hockey

1. **Pioneers of Women's Hockey**: Women have been playing hockey since the 1890s, but it wasn't until the 1990s that the sport gained major attention.

2. **First Women's World Championship**: The first official Women's World Championship was held in 1990, with Canada taking the gold.

3. **Olympic Debut**: Women's hockey made its Olympic debut in 1998, with the USA winning the first gold medal.

4. **USA vs. Canada Rivalry**: The USA and Canada have a fierce rivalry in women's hockey, often meeting in the finals of major tournaments.

5. **Hayley Wickenheiser's Legacy**: Wickenheiser is considered one of the greatest women's hockey players, winning four Olympic golds with Canada.

6. **Brianna Decker's Impact**: Decker has been a top player for the USA, known for her leadership and playmaking abilities.

7. **Marie-Philip Poulin - Captain Clutch**: Poulin scored game-winning goals for Canada in two Olympic gold medal games, earning her the nickname "Captain Clutch."

8. **Kendall Coyne's Speed**: Coyne competed in the NHL All-Star fastest skater competition, proving her speed rivals that of male players.

9. **Finland's Rise**: Finland has consistently been one of the top teams in women's hockey, often challenging the USA and Canada.

10. **CWHL and NWHL**: The Canadian Women's Hockey League (CWHL) and the National Women's Hockey

League (NWHL) have provided professional opportunities for female players.

11. **Ann-Renée Desbiens' Goalie Skills**: Known for her impressive saves, Desbiens has helped lead Canada to several major victories.

12. **Angela Ruggiero's Versatility**: Ruggiero played defense for Team USA in four Olympics and is known as one of the best to ever play the position.

13. **Japan's Determination**: Japan's women's team, known as "Smile Japan," has been making strides in international tournaments.

14. **Sweden's Silver Medal Surprise**: Sweden won silver in the 2006 Olympics, surprising the hockey world with their strong play.

15. **Gillian Apps - A Family Legacy**: Apps comes from a famous hockey family and won three Olympic golds with Canada.

16. **First Women's Outdoor Game**: In 2016, the NWHL held the first women's outdoor game, a big milestone for the sport.

17. **Sarah Nurse - Breaking Barriers**: Nurse became the first Black woman to play for Canada in the Olympics, inspiring young players everywhere.

18. **Cammi Granato - A Hall of Famer**: Granato was one of the first women inducted into the Hockey Hall of Fame, a major honor.

19. **Jayna Hefford's Scoring Record**: Hefford is one of Canada's top scorers in Olympic history, contributing to multiple gold medals.

20. **The PWHL's Future**: The new Professional Women's Hockey League (PWHL) aims to provide more opportunities for female players worldwide.

Chapter 16: Goalie Facts

1. **The Masked Man**: Jacques Plante was the first goalie to wear a mask during an NHL game in 1959 after taking a puck to the face. His innovation changed hockey forever.

2. **Butterfly Style**: Many goalies today use the "butterfly" style, dropping to their knees to cover the bottom of the net. Patrick Roy popularized this technique.

3. **Tallest Goalie**: Ben Bishop stands at 6'7", making him one of the tallest goalies in NHL history. His height helps him cover more of the net.

4. **Smallest Goalie**: Roy Worters, who played in the 1920s and 1930s, was only 5'3" but still won awards as one of the best goalies of his time.

5. **Most Career Wins**: Martin Brodeur holds the record for the most career wins by a goalie, with 691 victories.

6. **First Goalie Goal**: Ron Hextall became the first goalie to score a goal by shooting the puck directly into the other team's net in 1987.

7. **Most Shutouts in a Career**: Martin Brodeur also holds the record for the most career shutouts, with 125.

8. **The Goalie Stick Curve**: Goalie sticks have a slight curve to help them clear the puck away from the net. Some goalies have custom curves for their unique style.

9. **Most Saves in a Game**: Sam LoPresti made 80 saves in a single game in 1941—a record that still stands.

10. **Goalie Superstitions**: Many goalies are highly superstitious. Some have routines like tapping the posts a certain way before each period.

11. **The Goalie Crease**: The blue paint in front of the net is the goalie's "crease." Only the goalie is allowed inside this area, protecting them from interference.

12. **Goalie Gear Evolution**: In the early days, goalies wore almost no padding. Today's goalies wear specially designed gear that protects them from high-speed pucks.

13. **Youngest Goalie to Play**: Harry Lumley was only 17 when he played his first NHL game as a goalie, setting a record for the youngest netminder.

14. **Longest Goalie Streak**: Glenn Hall holds the record for the longest streak of consecutive games played by a goalie, at 502 games.

15. **Goalie Masks with Designs**: Goalies often personalize their masks with unique designs. Gerry Cheevers painted "stitches" on his mask to mark where he would have been injured without it.

16. **Most Saves in a Shutout**: Ben Scrivens made 59 saves in a shutout game in 2014, the most for any goalie in an NHL shutout.

17. **Quickest Reflexes**: Some goalies, like Dominik Hasek, were known for their lightning-fast reflexes, often making sprawling saves.

18. **First Goalie to Wear All White**: Jonas Hiller wore an all-white mask and gear to distract shooters, who claimed it made the net seem smaller.

19. **Playing the Puck**: Goalies like Martin Brodeur were so skilled at handling the puck that the NHL created a rule limiting where goalies can play it behind the net.

20. **The Shootout Specialist**: Henrik Lundqvist was known for his skill in shootouts, often using his quick reactions to stop one-on-one attempts.

Chapter 17: Evolution of Hockey Equipment

1. **Leather to Fiberglass**: Early hockey helmets were made from leather. Today, they're made from fiberglass and carbon fiber, offering much more protection.

2. **First Masked Goalie**: Jacques Plante wore the first goalie mask in 1959, marking a major change in hockey safety.

3. **The Wooden Stick**: Hockey sticks were originally made from solid wood. Modern sticks use carbon fiber, making them lighter and more durable.

4. **The Birth of the Slap Shot**: The introduction of the curved stick blade in the 1960s allowed players to develop the powerful slap shot.

5. **Hockey Gloves**: Early gloves were thin and offered little protection. Today's gloves have padding that protects players' hands from high-speed impacts.

6. **Goalie Pads**: Goalie pads were originally stuffed with deer hair. Now they use advanced materials to absorb impacts and protect goalies.

7. **First Visors**: Visors became popular in the 1970s, and today, most players wear them to protect their eyes from pucks and sticks.

8. **Synthetic Ice**: In recent years, synthetic ice has allowed players to train without needing a rink. It's not quite like real ice, but it helps for practice.

9. **The Evolution of Skates**: Skates have evolved from simple leather boots to advanced designs with ankle support and custom-fit features.

10. **Mouthguards**: Originally rare, mouthguards became standard equipment to protect players' teeth and reduce the risk of concussions.

11. **Goalie Catching Gloves**: Early catching gloves were more like baseball gloves. Today's gloves are larger, giving goalies more control in catching pucks.

12. **Pucks Frozen Before Games**: Freezing pucks reduces their bounce, making them easier to control on the ice.

13. **The Modern Face Shield**: Full face shields protect players from high sticks and pucks, especially in junior leagues where safety is key.

14. **Composite Sticks**: Carbon fiber composite sticks are lightweight and strong, allowing players to shoot faster and more accurately.

15. **The Chest Protector**: Goalie chest protectors used to be minimal. Today, they're designed to absorb impact, allowing goalies to block shots safely.

16. **The First Helmets**: Helmets became mandatory in the NHL in 1979, and players who wore them often felt safer and more protected.

17. **Custom Skates**: Some players use custom-molded skates to improve comfort and performance, a luxury early players didn't have.

18. **The Rise of Goalie Masks**: Goalies used to play without masks until the 1960s. Today, every goalie wears a mask with a unique design.

19. **Protective Neck Guards**: To protect from stray pucks and sticks, many players wear neck guards, especially goalies.

20. **Advancements in Shoulder Pads**: Shoulder pads used to be simple cloth with padding, but now they're high-tech pieces that absorb and distribute impact.

Chapter 18: Speed and Strength

1. **Fastest Skater**: Connor McDavid holds the title of one of the fastest skaters in the NHL, reaching speeds over 25 miles per hour!

2. **Hardest Shot**: Zdeno Chara recorded a 108.8 mph slap shot, setting the record for the hardest shot in the NHL.

3. **Longest Shift**: During the 2014 playoffs, Alex Ovechkin spent nearly two minutes on the ice in one shift, showcasing his endurance.

4. **Most Hits in a Game**: Cal Clutterbuck set a record with 19 hits in a single game, showing the physicality required in hockey.

5. **High-Speed Skating**: NHL players can reach speeds faster than most Olympic speed skaters, making them some of the fastest athletes on ice.

6. **Strongest Player**: Players like Milan Lucic are known for their strength, with the ability to overpower opponents in physical battles.

7. **Quick Reflexes**: Goalies like Dominik Hasek are famous for their quick reflexes, reacting to shots within fractions of a second.

8. **Endurance Training**: Hockey players train for endurance, often staying on the ice for 45-second shifts at top speed.

9. **Intense Workouts**: NHL players train with high-intensity workouts, including weightlifting, sprints, and agility drills.

10. **Body Checks**: A well-placed body check can stop an opponent from advancing, showing the power and control players must have.

11. **Powerful Legs**: Hockey players have strong legs to generate explosive speed, allowing them to skate faster and shoot harder.

12. **Box Jumps for Speed**: Box jumps are a common exercise for hockey players to develop explosive power and speed.

13. **Quick Footwork**: Skaters like Pavel Bure had lightning-fast footwork, making it hard for opponents to keep up.

14. **The Ironman Streak**: Doug Jarvis played 964 consecutive games, showing incredible durability and strength over his career.

15. **Strength in Scrums**: During puck battles, players must use their strength to gain control, often wrestling with opponents along the boards.

16. **Agility Drills**: Many players practice agility drills to improve their balance and movement on the ice.

17. **Cardio Conditioning**: Hockey players need high-level cardio fitness to handle the intense physical demands of the game.

18. **Stick Strength**: Players need strong wrists and forearms to shoot and control the puck effectively, especially under pressure.

19. **Hand-Eye Coordination**: Top players have excellent hand-eye coordination, allowing them to deflect pucks and make split-second plays.

20. **Flexibility for Goalies**: Goalies like Jonathan Quick are known for their flexibility, which helps them make saves in challenging positions.

Chapter 19: Penalties Explained

1. **What's a Power Play?**: When a player is sent to the penalty box, their team plays with one fewer player, giving the other team a "power play" advantage.

2. **The Penalty Box**: Players who break the rules sit in the "sin bin" or penalty box, away from the action for 2, 5, or even 10 minutes, depending on the penalty.

3. **Minor Penalties**: The most common penalty is a "minor," lasting two minutes, given for things like tripping or holding.

4. **Major Penalties**: Major penalties are for serious fouls, like fighting, and keep players in the box for five minutes.

5. **Fighting**: Believe it or not, fighting isn't always banned! Players who fight get a major penalty, but they can return to the game after serving time in the box.

6. **Double Minor**: Some penalties, like high-sticking that draws blood, result in a "double minor" with four minutes in the box.

7. **High-Sticking**: If a player's stick hits an opponent above the shoulders, they'll receive a high-sticking penalty.

8. **Hooking**: Using the stick to "hook" or pull back an opponent is against the rules and results in a two-minute penalty.

9. **Tripping**: Intentionally using the stick, leg, or arm to trip an opponent leads to a two-minute penalty.

10. **Holding**: Players aren't allowed to hold onto their opponents to prevent them from moving, leading to a holding penalty.

11. **Cross-Checking**: Shoving an opponent with the stick held in both hands is called cross-checking, which is illegal and results in a penalty.

12. **Slashing**: When a player swings their stick at an opponent, it's called slashing. If it's forceful, it leads to a penalty.

13. **Interference**: Interference happens when a player blocks or hits an opponent who doesn't have the puck.

14. **Delay of Game**: If a player shoots the puck out of play without it deflecting off anyone, they receive a delay of game penalty.

15. **Goalie Interference**: Players can't touch or interfere with the goalie in the crease, or they'll get a penalty.

16. **Too Many Men**: When a team has more players on the ice than allowed, they receive a penalty called "too many men."

17. **Boarding**: Boarding is when a player dangerously shoves an opponent into the boards, resulting in a penalty.

18. **Spearing**: Jabbing an opponent with the blade of the stick is called spearing and is a serious offense with a major penalty.

19. **Penalty Shot**: If a player is fouled while on a breakaway, they may be awarded a penalty shot, allowing them to take a free shot on goal.

20. **Game Misconduct**: For very serious infractions, a player may receive a game misconduct, meaning they're ejected from the game.

Chapter 20: Hockey Rules

1. **Offside**: Players can't enter the offensive zone (past the blue line) before the puck. If they do, it's called offside, and play stops.

2. **Icing the Puck**: Icing occurs when a player shoots the puck from their side of the rink all the way past the opponent's goal line. This results in a face-off in the shooter's defensive zone.

3. **Face-Offs**: A face-off occurs to start play, with two players battling for control of the puck after it's dropped by the referee.

4. **Goal Crease**: Only the goalie can stay inside the blue-painted crease, and opposing players aren't allowed to interfere with them in this space.

5. **Goal Scoring**: For a goal to count, the puck must completely cross the goal line. Even a fraction of an inch counts!

6. **Penalty Kill**: When a team is shorthanded due to a penalty, they're on a "penalty kill," defending against the opponent's power play.

7. **Four-on-Four**: When both teams have players in the penalty box, the game becomes four-on-four, opening up more space on the ice.

8. **Delayed Penalty**: When a penalty is called against a team, play continues until the other team touches the puck, allowing them a chance to score with an extra attacker.

9. **Shootout**: If the game is tied after overtime, teams go to a shootout, where players take turns trying to score one-on-one against the goalie.

10. **Overtime**: If a game is tied at the end of regulation, it goes into overtime, with the first team to score winning the game.

11. **Checking**: Body checking is allowed in hockey, but only to a player who has the puck. Illegal hits result in penalties.

12. **Line Changes**: Teams can swap players on the fly during play, a unique feature of hockey that keeps the game fast-paced.

13. **Power Play Lineup**: Teams often use their best players on the power play, arranging them to maximize their chance of scoring.

14. **Clearing the Puck**: Defenders often "clear" the puck from their zone by sending it all the way to the other end to relieve pressure.

15. **Penalty Kill Strategy**: Teams on the penalty kill often use a diamond or box formation to protect their net and block shots.

16. **One-Timer Shot**: A one-timer happens when a player takes a shot right off a pass without stopping the puck, adding power and surprise.

17. **Pulling the Goalie**: Near the end of a game, if a team is losing, they might "pull the goalie" to add an extra skater, hoping to tie the game.

18. **Hand Passes**: Players aren't allowed to pass the puck to teammates with their hands, except when in the defensive zone.

19. **Drop Pass**: A player skating with the puck can leave it behind for a teammate to pick up, a move called a "drop pass."

20. **Zamboni Resurface**: Between periods, the Zamboni resurfaces the ice to ensure smooth skating conditions for players.

Chapter 21: Hockey Training Drills

1. **Skating Sprints**: Players practice skating as fast as possible in short bursts, improving their speed on the ice.

2. **Stickhandling Drills**: Players practice weaving the puck around cones to improve their control and hand-eye coordination.

3. **Shooting Accuracy**: Players aim at targets in the net to improve shooting accuracy, a key skill for scoring goals.

4. **Passing Practice**: Passing drills help players work on precision and timing, allowing for smooth team play.

5. **One-Timer Practice**: Players practice taking shots directly off a pass, adding power and speed to their shots.

6. **Power Skating**: Power skating drills focus on strong strides, helping players generate speed and power.

7. **Backward Skating**: Defensemen often practice skating backward, crucial for maintaining control while defending against attackers.

8. **Breakout Drills**: Teams practice breaking out of their defensive zone with quick passes and coordinated movement.

9. **Shot Blocking**: Players practice positioning and techniques for blocking shots, a skill often used by defensemen.

10. **Tip-In Drills**: Players practice deflecting pucks in front of the net to create unexpected scoring chances.

11. **Face-Off Practice**: Centers work on winning face-offs by practicing different techniques for gaining control of the puck.

12. **Passing in Tight Spaces**: Passing in close quarters helps players make quick, accurate passes under pressure.

13. **Penalty Kill Drills**: Teams practice playing short-handed, focusing on positioning and blocking shots to kill penalties.

14. **Forechecking Practice**: Forechecking drills help players pressure the opponent's defense to regain control of the puck.

15. **Goalie Reflex Drills**: Goalies practice reacting to fast, unexpected shots to improve their quickness and reflexes.

16. **Deke Moves**: Players work on faking out opponents by practicing deke moves, adding unpredictability to their game.

17. **Rebound Drills**: Players practice taking quick shots off rebounds, ready to capitalize on loose pucks around the net.

18. **Agility Drills**: Cone drills help players work on their agility and turning ability, allowing them to maneuver quickly on the ice.

19. **Small-Area Games**: Coaches set up small-area games to help players practice passing, shooting, and defense in tight spaces.

20. **Conditioning Drills**: Players finish practice with conditioning drills like laps and sprints to build endurance.

Chapter 22: Rookie Success Stories

1. **Wayne Gretzky's First Season**: In his first season, Gretzky scored 137 points, showing the world he was destined for greatness.

2. **Mario Lemieux's Debut Goal**: Mario Lemieux scored on his first NHL shift, making an immediate impact on the league.

3. **Sidney Crosby's Rookie Season**: Crosby scored 102 points in his first season, living up to the hype as "The Next One."
4. **Teemu Selanne's Record**: Selanne scored 76 goals as a rookie, a record that still stands and is unlikely to be broken.
5. **Alexander Ovechkin's Debut**: Ovechkin scored two goals in his first game and won the Calder Trophy as Rookie of the Year.
6. **Ken Dryden's Playoff Debut**: Dryden won the Conn Smythe Trophy as playoff MVP in his rookie season, leading the Canadiens to a Stanley Cup.
7. **Bobby Orr's Rookie Defense**: Orr revolutionized defense in his first year, showing his incredible skating and scoring skills.
8. **Evgeni Malkin's Goal Streak**: Malkin scored a goal in each of his first six NHL games, the longest streak by a rookie.
9. **Connor McDavid's Rookie Points**: Despite missing games due to injury, McDavid finished with 48 points, proving his skill.

10. **Auston Matthews' Four-Goal Debut**: Matthews scored four goals in his first NHL game, an incredible achievement for a rookie.

11. **Nathan MacKinnon's Rookie Speed**: MacKinnon's speed and scoring ability earned him the Calder Trophy as Rookie of the Year.

12. **Patrick Kane's Rookie Playmaking**: Kane's vision and playmaking abilities helped him rack up 72 points in his first season.

13. **Marty Brodeur's Goalie Skills**: Brodeur earned a playoff spot for the Devils as a rookie and went on to have an incredible career.

14. **Sergei Makarov's Rookie Scoring**: Makarov scored 86 points as a 31-year-old rookie, winning the Calder Trophy.

15. **Mathew Barzal's Speedy Points**: Barzal's quickness and creativity led to a 85-point rookie season, winning him the Calder Trophy.

16. **Joe Nieuwendyk's 51 Goals**: Nieuwendyk scored 51 goals as a rookie, showing his natural scoring talent.

17. **Dale Hawerchuk's 100 Points**: Hawerchuk scored 103 points in his rookie season, making him an instant star for the Winnipeg Jets.

18. **Steve Mason's Goalie Wins**: Mason won 33 games as a rookie goalie, helping Columbus make the playoffs for the first time.

19. **Cale Makar's Rookie Defense**: Makar's outstanding two-way play earned him the Calder Trophy as the NHL's top rookie.

20. **Kirill Kaprizov's Debut Spark**: Kaprizov scored 51 points in his rookie season, reigniting excitement for hockey in Minnesota.

Chapter 23: Coaches and Strategies

1. **Scotty Bowman - The Winningest Coach**: Scotty Bowman is the winningest coach in NHL history, with nine Stanley Cups across three different teams.

2. **Jacques Lemaire and the Trap**: Lemaire popularized the "neutral zone trap," a defensive strategy that clogs up the middle of the ice, making it hard for opponents to advance.

3. **Mike Babcock's Discipline**: Known for his structured approach, Babcock emphasizes discipline and teamwork, leading to Olympic golds and a Stanley Cup.

4. **Herb Brooks' Miracle**: Brooks famously coached the 1980 U.S. Olympic team to victory over the Soviet Union in the "Miracle on Ice."

5. **Pat Burns' Defensive Style**: Burns' teams were known for their tough, defensive play, helping him win the Jack Adams Award as Coach of the Year three times.

6. **Ken Hitchcock's Focus on Defense**: Hitchcock's coaching philosophy centers on defense-first hockey,

and he led the Dallas Stars to a Stanley Cup with this approach.

7. **Barry Trotz's Islander Transformation**: Trotz turned the Islanders into one of the league's best defensive teams, helping them reach the playoffs consistently.

8. **Dan Bylsma's Offensive Plays**: Bylsma coached the Pittsburgh Penguins to a Stanley Cup with an emphasis on speed and offensive creativity.

9. **Darryl Sutter's Gritty Style**: Known for his demanding approach, Sutter led the Los Angeles Kings to two Stanley Cups with hard-hitting, defensive play.

10. **Glen Sather's Star-Studded Lineups**: Sather's ability to coach star-studded rosters helped the Edmonton Oilers win multiple Stanley Cups in the '80s.

11. **Joel Quenneville's Systems**: Quenneville's structured systems and attention to detail helped the Chicago Blackhawks win three Stanley Cups.

12. **Claude Julien's Balanced Strategy**: Julien's focus on balanced offense and defense led the Boston Bruins to a Stanley Cup in 2011.

13. **Mike Keenan's Fiery Style**: Known for his intense personality, Keenan pushed players to their limits and led the Rangers to a Stanley Cup in 1994.

14. **Toe Blake's Legacy**: Toe Blake coached the Montreal Canadiens to eight Stanley Cups, making him one of the most successful coaches in history.

15. **Al Arbour's Leadership**: Arbour led the New York Islanders to four consecutive Stanley Cups with a team-first mentality.

16. **Paul Maurice's Adjustments**: Known for adapting his strategies, Maurice has been able to guide teams through playoff runs with various game plans.

17. **Phil Jackson's Mental Approach**: Jackson's unique mental and motivational techniques inspired his teams to perform at their best.

18. **Ron Wilson's Special Teams**: Wilson's focus on special teams made his power plays and penalty kills some of the best in the league.

19. **Guy Carbonneau's Defensive Focus**: Carbonneau's defense-first approach helped him lead successful penalty kills and protect leads.

20. **Gerard Gallant's Player Connection**: Gallant's ability to connect with players helped the Vegas Golden Knights reach the Stanley Cup Final in their first season.

Chapter 24: Officiating in Hockey

1. **Referees and Linesmen**: Hockey games have two referees and two linesmen who monitor the game, calling penalties and making sure the rules are followed.

2. **The Orange Armband**: Only referees wear orange armbands to show they're the ones responsible for calling penalties.

3. **Linesmen's Duties**: Linesmen focus on offside and icing calls but can also break up fights and assist with penalty calls if needed.

4. **The Goal Judge**: In the past, a goal judge sat behind the net to turn on a red light when a goal was scored. Now, it's mostly handled by video review.

5. **Video Review**: Video review helps officials make sure all goals are legitimate, preventing mistakes on critical plays.

6. **The Challenge System**: Coaches can challenge certain calls, like offside or goalie interference, if they believe the officials made a mistake.

7. **Icing Calls**: Linesmen determine icing when the puck crosses the red line without touching another player, leading to a face-off in the defensive zone.

8. **Offside Reviews**: Offside reviews ensure that goals aren't scored after an offside, keeping the game fair.

9. **Penalty Enforcement**: Referees decide whether infractions are minor or major penalties, impacting the time players spend in the penalty box.

10. **Delayed Penalty Signal**: Referees signal a delayed penalty by raising their arm, allowing play to continue until the offending team gains possession.

11. **Hand Passes**: Officials call hand passes if a player uses their hand to pass the puck to a teammate in the offensive zone.

12. **Face-Off Fairness**: Referees ensure that players line up fairly during face-offs, ensuring no one gets an unfair advantage.

13. **Broken Stick Rules**: Players aren't allowed to play with a broken stick, and referees enforce this rule for safety.

14. **Too Many Men**: If a team has too many players on the ice, referees call a penalty for "too many men," leading to a power play.

15. **Goalie Interference**: Referees carefully watch for goalie interference, ensuring players don't obstruct the goalie's ability to make a save.

16. **Diving Penalties**: Players who "dive" or exaggerate a fall to draw a penalty can be penalized for unsportsmanlike conduct.

17. **The Fight Break-Up**: When fights occur, officials allow a few moments before stepping in to break it up, ensuring safety for both players.

18. **End of Period Signal**: Officials signal the end of a period by blowing the whistle and ensuring both teams return to their benches.

19. **High-Sticking Injuries**: Referees watch for high-sticking penalties that draw blood, resulting in a double-minor penalty.

20. **Game Misconduct Ejections**: For serious fouls, officials can give a game misconduct penalty, ejecting a player from the game.

Chapter 25: Ice Maintenance

1. **The Role of the Zamboni**: The Zamboni resurfaces the ice between periods, ensuring a smooth playing surface for players.

2. **Layered Ice Creation**: Ice rinks are created by spraying thin layers of water, allowing each layer to freeze before the next is added.

3. **Ice Thickness**: NHL ice is usually about 1 inch thick, maintained by a refrigeration system beneath the rink.

4. **Cold Temperatures**: Rinks are kept around 16°F (-9°C) to keep the ice solid and prevent it from melting.

5. **Painting the Ice**: The white color of the ice is painted on, along with the lines, circles, and logos, all beneath the top layer of ice.

6. **Water Quality**: High-quality, filtered water is used to ensure the ice remains clear and smooth, free of impurities.

7. **Zamboni Blade**: The Zamboni's sharp blade shaves off the top layer of ice, removing grooves and scratches.

8. **Hot Water Resurfacing**: Hot water is used to resurface the ice because it freezes more smoothly than cold water.

9. **Dry Scraping**: Some arenas use a dry scrape before the final Zamboni pass to clear away loose ice shavings.

10. **Ice Edging**: An edger trims the edges of the ice, ensuring the boards and corners are as smooth as the center.

11. **Goal Crease Maintenance**: The goal crease area is scraped and maintained more frequently, as it takes a lot of wear and tear from skates.

12. **Back-to-Back Games**: During tournaments or doubleheaders, ice crews work overtime to keep the rink smooth and playable.

13. **Repairing Divots**: Ice maintenance crews fill in divots caused by skates, ensuring the ice stays level.

14. **Humidity Control**: Keeping humidity low in rinks prevents the ice from becoming soft or slushy.

15. **Outdoor Game Challenges**: Outdoor games require extra care, with ice crews battling sun, wind, and temperature changes.

16. **Water Tank Capacity**: The Zamboni holds up to 200 gallons of water, enough to resurface the entire rink.

17. **Ice Melting and Rebuilding**: At the end of the season, the ice is melted down and rebuilt the next year with fresh layers.

18. **Blue Line Precision**: The blue lines must be perfectly straight and even, as they're important for making offside calls.

19. **Crease Color Touch-Ups**: The blue crease is touched up regularly to keep it visible and clear for players and officials.

20. **Safety First**: Ice maintenance ensures that players can skate safely, without worrying about tripping on bumps or cracks.

Chapter 26: Famous Hockey Arenas

1. **Madison Square Garden**: Known as "The Garden," MSG is one of the most famous arenas, home to the New York Rangers.
2. **Bell Centre**: Home to the Montreal Canadiens, Bell Centre is known for its passionate fans and electric atmosphere.
3. **Scotiabank Arena**: The Toronto Maple Leafs play at Scotiabank Arena, one of the most iconic spots in Canadian hockey.
4. **United Center**: United Center in Chicago is home to the Blackhawks, known for its loud "Chelsea Dagger" goal song.
5. **Rogers Place**: This high-tech arena in Edmonton features an impressive scoreboard and hosts the Oilers.
6. **Staples Center**: The Los Angeles Kings play at the Staples Center, where fans can watch hockey right in the heart of LA.
7. **Xcel Energy Center**: Known for its "State of Hockey" pride, the Xcel Energy Center is home to the Minnesota Wild.
8. **T-Mobile Arena**: Located in Las Vegas, T-Mobile Arena is home to the Golden Knights, with unique pre-game shows.
9. **Little Caesars Arena**: The Detroit Red Wings play at this modern arena with a rich history tied to Hockeytown, USA.

10. **PNC Arena**: Known for its "Storm Surge" celebrations, PNC Arena is home to the Carolina Hurricanes.
11. **Amalie Arena**: The Tampa Bay Lightning's arena is known for its lively atmosphere, especially during playoff season.
12. **Canadian Tire Centre**: Ottawa Senators fans cheer at the Canadian Tire Centre, which celebrates the spirit of Canadian hockey.
13. **KeyBank Center**: Home to the Buffalo Sabres, KeyBank Center is known for its dedicated fan base.
14. **Bridgestone Arena**: Nashville Predators fans bring country music vibes to hockey games at Bridgestone Arena.
15. **BB&T Center**: The Florida Panthers play at BB&T Center, representing hockey in a warm-weather state.
16. **SAP Center**: Known as "The Shark Tank," SAP Center is home to the San Jose Sharks.
17. **Gila River Arena**: The Arizona Coyotes play at Gila River Arena, where fans enjoy hockey in the desert.
18. **Pepsi Center**: Home to the Colorado Avalanche, Pepsi Center is known for its enthusiastic Denver crowd.
19. **TD Garden**: Boston's TD Garden is home to the Bruins, where fans bring serious energy to every game.
20. **The Forum (Old Montreal Forum)**: Before moving to Bell Centre, the Canadiens played here, and it's considered one of the most legendary hockey arenas in history.

Chapter 27: Hockey Rink Dimensions

1. **NHL Rink Size**: NHL rinks are 200 feet long and 85 feet wide. This standard size is used for all North American professional games.

2. **Olympic Rink Size**: Olympic and international rinks are larger, at 200 feet long and 100 feet wide, giving players more space to maneuver.

3. **Goal Crease Dimensions**: The goalie's crease is 8 feet wide and 4 feet deep, providing a protective area for the goalie.

4. **Face-Off Circles**: Each of the five face-off circles has a 15-foot diameter, giving players space to battle for the puck.

5. **Neutral Zone**: The area between the two blue lines is called the neutral zone. It's typically 50 feet wide in an NHL rink.

6. **Goal Line**: The goal line is set 11 feet from the end boards and is crucial for determining goals and icing calls.

7. **Blue Lines**: Each blue line is 12 inches wide and divides the rink into three zones: offensive, defensive, and neutral.

8. **Red Line**: The red line splits the rink in half and is used to judge icing and offside calls.

9. **Face-Off Spots**: There are nine face-off spots on the rink, where referees drop the puck to start play.

10. **Corners**: The rounded corners of the rink help keep the puck in play by making it bounce around smoothly.

11. **Boards Height**: The boards around the rink are typically 42 inches high to protect fans and keep the puck in play.

12. **Glass Height**: Plexiglass extends 5-6 feet above the boards to protect fans and players from flying pucks.

13. **Penalty Boxes**: Each side of the rink has a penalty box for players who need to serve penalties. These are located next to the team benches.

14. **Bench Areas**: The players' benches are positioned along the boards on either side of the rink, allowing quick line changes.

15. **Zamboni Entrance**: A designated area along the boards allows the Zamboni to enter and resurface the ice.

16. **Spectator Netting**: Behind each goal, netting is installed to protect fans from high-flying pucks.

17. **Face-Off Dots**: The center face-off dot and the four face-off dots in each zone are used to align players for face-offs.

18. **Dasher Boards**: The lower portion of the boards is padded and painted yellow, known as the dasher, to protect players during checks.

19. **Penalty Bench Dimensions**: The penalty bench is about 6 feet wide, allowing room for players to sit while serving penalties.

20. **Ice Thickness**: The ice is typically kept at around 1 inch thick, maintained by the refrigeration system below the rink.

Chapter 28: Statistics and Records

1. **Most Career Points**: Wayne Gretzky holds the record for most points in NHL history with 2,857, a number no one has come close to.

2. **Most Goals in a Season**: Gretzky also set the record for the most goals in a season with 92 in 1981-82.

3. **Most Assists in a Career**: Gretzky holds the record for assists, too, with 1,963, showing his playmaking skill.

4. **Most Shutouts in a Career**: Martin Brodeur recorded 125 shutouts, the highest by any goalie in NHL history.

5. **Most Penalty Minutes**: Dave "Tiger" Williams holds the record for most penalty minutes with 3,966 over his career.

6. **Most Wins by a Goalie**: Martin Brodeur also holds the record for the most wins by a goalie, with 691 career victories.

7. **Longest Winning Streak**: The Pittsburgh Penguins won 17 consecutive games in 1992-93, setting a record for the longest winning streak.

8. **Most Games Played**: Patrick Marleau played 1,779 games, breaking Gordie Howe's record for most NHL games played.

9. **Most Stanley Cups Won**: Henri Richard of the Montreal Canadiens won 11 Stanley Cups, the most by any player.

10. **Most Consecutive Playoff Appearances**: The Boston Bruins made 29 consecutive playoff appearances from 1968 to 1996, a league record.

11. **Most Goals by a Defenseman**: Paul Coffey scored 48 goals in the 1985-86 season, setting a record for defensemen.

12. **Most Points by a Rookie**: Teemu Selanne scored 132 points in his rookie season, including 76 goals, setting a high bar for newcomers.

13. **Most Points in a Game**: Darryl Sittler scored 10 points in a single game in 1976, a record that still stands.

14. **Most Goals in a Playoff Season**: Reggie Leach scored 19 goals in the 1975-76 playoffs, setting a record for postseason goals.

15. **Fastest Hat Trick**: Bill Mosienko scored three goals in 21 seconds in 1952, achieving the fastest hat trick in NHL history.

16. **Most Power-Play Goals in a Season**: Tim Kerr scored 34 power-play goals in a single season in 1985-86.

17. **Most Short-Handed Goals**: Wayne Gretzky holds the record for most short-handed goals with 73 in his career.

18. **Most Saves in a Game**: Sam LoPresti made 80 saves in a game in 1941, a record for the most saves in a single game.

19. **Longest Game Played**: In 1936, the Red Wings and Maroons played the longest NHL game, lasting over 176 minutes.

20. **Most Game-Winning Goals**: Jaromir Jagr scored 135 game-winning goals, the highest by any player.

Chapter 29: Future of Hockey

1. **Rising Star - Connor Bedard**: Many believe Connor Bedard will be the next big thing in hockey, with incredible skill even at a young age.

2. **Increased Use of Analytics**: Teams are using more data and analytics to make decisions, tracking every pass, shot, and goal to improve performance.

3. **Advancements in Equipment**: Hockey equipment continues to evolve, with lighter and more protective gear designed to keep players safe.

4. **Women's Hockey Growth**: Women's hockey is gaining popularity, with more leagues and events providing opportunities for female athletes.

5. **Expansion to New Markets**: The NHL is expanding to new cities and countries, introducing hockey to places where it's less popular.

6. **Sustainable Rinks**: More rinks are being built with eco-friendly materials and energy-efficient technology to reduce environmental impact.

7. **Innovations in Fan Engagement**: From virtual reality experiences to interactive apps, fans can connect with the game like never before.

8. **3-on-3 Overtime**: The NHL introduced 3-on-3 overtime to make games more exciting, and it's quickly become a fan favorite.

9. **Youth Development Programs**: More youth hockey programs are emerging, making the sport accessible to more kids and growing the talent pool.

10. **Growing Popularity of Inline Hockey**: Inline hockey is becoming more popular, allowing people to play hockey year-round, even in warm climates.

11. **International Leagues**: Leagues in countries like China and South Korea are growing, introducing hockey to new parts of the world.

12. **Emerging Technologies in Training**: Tools like virtual reality and advanced tracking systems are being used to help players improve.

13. **Hybrid Icing Rule**: The hybrid icing rule is intended to protect players from high-speed collisions while maintaining the pace of the game.

14. **Diversity in Hockey**: More players from diverse backgrounds are entering the NHL, making hockey a more inclusive sport.

15. **Player Safety Advances**: New rules and better equipment are being developed to protect players from injuries, especially concussions.

16. **Global Hockey Tournaments**: Plans are underway to introduce new global hockey tournaments, like a World Cup-style competition.

17. **Smart Puck Technology**: The NHL has experimented with smart pucks that track movement, speed, and other data to enhance broadcasting.

18. **Increased Media Coverage**: Women's hockey and junior leagues are getting more media coverage, expanding their fan base.

19. **New Expansion Teams**: Following the success of teams like the Vegas Golden Knights and Seattle Kraken, more cities may get their own teams.

20. **Hockey's Olympic Future**: With ongoing debates, the NHL's participation in future Olympics remains a hot

topic, especially for fans who love international competition.

Bonus Chapter: More Cool Fun Facts from the Hockey World

1. **The "Original Six"**: The NHL's "Original Six" teams— Boston Bruins, Chicago Blackhawks, Detroit Red Wings, Montreal Canadiens, New York Rangers, and Toronto Maple Leafs—are the oldest teams in the league and built much of hockey's early history.

2. **The Golden Puck**: In Finland, the Golden Puck is awarded to the best Finnish player of the season, similar to the NHL's Hart Trophy.

3. **Hockey in Space**: Astronauts played a mini game of hockey on the International Space Station, using a puck that floated in zero gravity!

4. **The Oldest Ice Hockey Puck**: The oldest known ice hockey puck was found in Canada and is estimated to be over 200 years old.

5. **Longest Continuous Game**: In 2015, Canadian players set a record by playing a hockey game that lasted over 250 hours straight to raise money for charity!

6. **The Stanley Cup Mistake**: A mistake on the Stanley Cup misspelled the Toronto Maple Leafs as the "Toronto Maple Leaes" in 1962—it's still there today.

7. **The French Connection Line**: The Buffalo Sabres' famous line in the 1970s, known as the "French Connection," was one of the most celebrated in NHL history, named after the players' French-Canadian heritage.

8. **Mascots in the NHL**: Not all NHL teams have mascots. The New York Rangers and Seattle Kraken are two teams that don't have an official mascot.

9. **The Frozen Four**: The NCAA's men's hockey championship is called the "Frozen Four," mirroring college basketball's Final Four.

10. **Fastest Ice Resurfacing**: The fastest Zamboni run recorded was under 9 minutes, a feat to get the ice ready for play again quickly.

11. **First Asian NHL Player**: Larry Kwong was the first player of Asian descent to play in the NHL when he skated for the New York Rangers in 1948.

12. **The Lucky Loonie**: Before the 2002 Olympics, Canadian officials buried a loonie (Canadian dollar coin) under the center ice as a good luck charm—and Canada went on to win gold.

13. **Australia's Ice Hockey League**: Yes, Australia has an ice hockey league, the AIHL, where fans cheer on teams like the Melbourne Ice and the Sydney Bears.

14. **"Hockey Night in Canada"**: Canada's iconic "Hockey Night in Canada" broadcast started in 1952, making it one of the longest-running TV shows in the world.

15. **First Outdoor Game**: The first NHL outdoor game was held in 2003 between the Edmonton Oilers and Montreal Canadiens, sparking the popular Winter Classic series.

16. **Hockey and Golf Crossover**: Many hockey players enjoy golf in the offseason. Hall of Famer Joe Sakic is known for his golf skills, even competing in pro-am tournaments.

17. **The Green Men**: Vancouver Canucks fans known as "The Green Men" gained fame by wearing full green bodysuits and taunting players in the penalty box.

18. **Hockey on Wheels**: Inline hockey, or roller hockey, is a popular version of the game played on pavement or gym floors worldwide, especially in warm climates.

19. **The First Hat Trick**: The term "hat trick" originated in 1946 when a Toronto hat shop owner rewarded a player who scored three goals in a game by giving him a free hat.

20. **The Stanley Cup Lost and Found**: The Stanley Cup has gone missing multiple times throughout history, once left on the side of the road and even found at the bottom of Mario Lemieux's pool!

21. **Goalie Goofs**: Some goalies have their own blooper reels for scoring on themselves or tripping in hilarious ways—it's all in good fun!

22. **The KHL's Largest Rink**: The Kontinental Hockey League (KHL) in Russia plays on the largest rinks in professional hockey, giving players more space to skate and strategize.

23. **Fastest Hockey Game Ever**: The shortest game on record was under 30 minutes due to a team not

showing up. They forfeited, so it went down as a super quick "victory."

24. **The Golden Knights' Lucky Charm**: The Vegas Golden Knights have "Chance," a neon green Gila monster mascot, who became a fan favorite with his quirky antics.

25. **Hockey Super Fans**: Some fans travel to every single game their team plays during a season. Known as "road warriors," these fans are incredibly dedicated.

26. **World's Largest Stick**: The world's largest hockey stick and puck, over 205 feet long, is on display in Duncan, British Columbia, Canada.

27. **Hockey Puck Temperature**: Pucks are frozen before games to keep them from bouncing. They start at about -10°F!

28. **Unique Hockey Trophy**: The "Toilet Bowl" is a unique, tongue-in-cheek trophy awarded at some youth tournaments to the last-place team.

29. **The NHL's Longest Road Trip**: The Vancouver Canucks often have the longest road trips in the NHL due to their remote location on the west coast.

30. **Hockey's Place in the Dictionary**: The word "hockey" is believed to come from the old French word "hoquet," meaning shepherd's stick.

31. **Ice Hockey's Popularity in India**: India has a growing ice hockey scene, with the Himalayan town of Leh hosting the country's first-ever ice hockey rink.

32. **The EBUG Rule**: "Emergency Backup Goalie" (EBUG) allows teams to use any qualified goalie in the stands if their regular goalies are unavailable, leading to memorable moments.

33. **The "Triple Gold Club"**: Only a few players have won Olympic gold, World Championship gold, and a Stanley Cup, joining the prestigious "Triple Gold Club."

34. **Stanley Cup Superstitions**: It's a common superstition that players won't touch the Stanley Cup unless they win it themselves.

35. **The Finnish "Sisu"**: Finnish players are known for their "sisu," a word meaning grit, courage, and determination, traits highly valued in hockey.

36. **First Hockey Movie**: The first hockey-themed movie was "The Hockey Champ," a 1939 Disney cartoon featuring Donald Duck!

37. **Longest Winning Streak by a Women's Team**: The Minnesota Golden Gophers women's team holds the record with 62 consecutive wins.

38. **Japan's Hockey History**: Japan has a long hockey history and even played in the 1936 Olympics, making it one of the oldest hockey programs outside North America and Europe.

39. **Zamboni Rides for Fans**: Some arenas let fans take a ride on the Zamboni during intermission, a unique experience that makes hockey games even more memorable.

40. **Hockey in Dubai**: Dubai, known for its deserts, also has ice hockey, with a rink inside the Dubai Mall and a growing fan base for the game.

THE END!

Made in United States
Orlando, FL
27 November 2024

54576345R00068